Table of Contents

D1401590

Rourke
Educational Media
rourkeeducationalmedia.com

Can you find these words?

flower

leaves

root

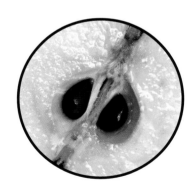

seeds

Fruit or Vegetable?

Fruits and vegetables are parts of plants.

Fruits hold the **seeds** of a plant.

seeds

Apples hold seeds. They are fruits.

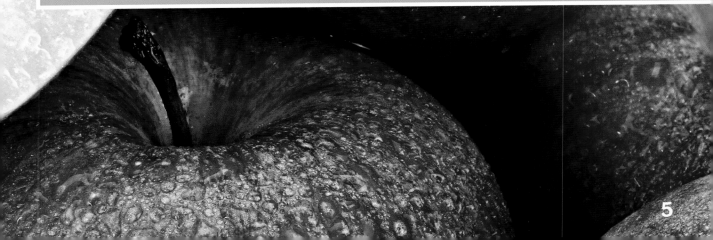

Oranges hold seeds.

They are fruits.

Vegetables are other plant parts.

Carrots are vegetables.
We eat the **root**.

root

Broccoli is a vegetable.

flower

We eat the **flower.**

Spinach is a vegetable.

leaves

We eat the **leaves**.

Did you find these words?

We eat the **flower**.

We eat the **leaves**.

We eat the **root**.

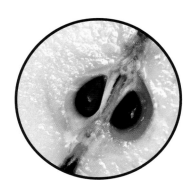

Fruits hold the **seeds** of a plant.

Photo Glossary

 **flower** (FLOU-uhr): The blossom of a plant that produces seeds or fruits.

 **leaves** (leevs): Flat, usually green structures that grow from a tree or plant.

 **root** (root): The part of a plant or tree that grows underground and collects water and nutrients.

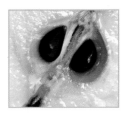 **seeds** (seeds): The parts of a flowering plant from which a new plant can grow.

Index

About the Author

Charlotte Hunter writes books about everything from friendship to fruit. When she's not writing, she enjoys going for long walks with her dog, Penny.

© 2019 Rourke Educational Media

www.rourkeeducationalmedia.com

PHOTO CREDITS: Cover: ©Steve Ross, ©Chunumunu; p.2,10-11,14,15: ©EVGENIYA68; p.2,12-13,14,15: ©Deyan Georgiev; p.2,4-5,14,15: ©hacohob; p.3: ©Kyu Oh; p.6-7: ©Dmetalfinch

Edited by: Keli Sipperley
Cover and interior design by: Rhea Magaro-Wallace

Library of Congress PCN Data
Fruit or Vegetable? / Charlotte Hunter
(Plants, Animals, and People)
ISBN (hard cover)(alk. paper) 978-1-64156-158-7
ISBN (soft cover) 978-1-64156-214-0
ISBN (e-Book) 978-1-64156-269-0
Library of Congress Control Number: 2017957770

Printed in the United States of America, North Mankato, Minnesota